Digital Products on Etsy:

How to Make Money Selling

Your Digital Products

Digital Products on Etsy:

How to Make Money Selling

Your Digital Products

Jose Valladares

About the Author:

I'm a multidisciplinary author with a deep curiosity for the world. With a degree in physics, chemistry, and mathematics, I have devoted my life to exploring the mysteries of the universe and seeking to understand the fundamental laws that govern our existence.

However, my interests extend far beyond the scientific realm. I am also an accomplished musician, having released nine albums that showcase my passion for playing the piano. When not writing or playing music, I devote time to prayer, seeking spiritual guidance and inspiration from our Lord Jesus.

As a prolific author, I have published over 46 books that cover a diverse range of topics, from coloring books, poetry, philosophy, music, science and spirituality to personal growth and transformation. My aim as a writer is to spread positivity and love, and to motivate others to live their best lives.

Currently residing in the dynamic city of Los Angeles, California, I am eager to connect with readers like you and embark on a journey of discovery and growth together.

Preface:

Welcome to the world of selling digital products on Etsy! This book is a comprehensive guide that will teach you everything you need to know about creating, listing, and promoting digital products on Etsy, as well as managing orders and scaling your business.

In today's digital age, the demand for digital products has increased rapidly, and Etsy provides an excellent platform for sellers to offer their unique creations to a global audience. Whether you are a seasoned Etsy seller or just starting out, this book will provide valuable insights and strategies to help you succeed in the competitive world of online sales.

In this book, we will cover topics such as setting up an Etsy shop, creating digital products, listing and promoting products, managing orders and customer relationships, and scaling and growing an Etsy shop. Each chapter is designed to provide practical advice and actionable steps to help you achieve your selling goals.

As a digital product seller on Etsy, you have the potential to earn a significant income while doing something that you love. With the right tools and knowledge, you can turn your passion into a successful business. This book will help you do just that.

I hope you find this book informative and inspiring, and I wish you all the best in your Etsy selling journey.

Introduction

Making Money Selling Digital Items on Etsy

The rise of the digital age has created new opportunities for creative entrepreneurs to make money selling digital products, and Etsy is one of the most popular platforms for doing so. Selling digital items on Etsy can be a great way to earn extra income or start a full-time business, and it offers a number of benefits over traditional selling methods. With low overhead costs, a large and engaged customer base, and the ability to sell products around the world, Etsy can provide a lucrative and rewarding opportunity for those willing to put in the effort. This book will provide readers with a comprehensive guide to making money selling digital items on Etsy, from getting started on the platform to scaling and growing their businesses.

Benefits of Selling Digital Products on Etsy

Selling digital products on Etsy has become an increasingly popular way for creative entrepreneurs to earn money online. There are numerous benefits to selling digital products on Etsy, which makes it an attractive option for those looking to start or grow their online business.

One of the primary benefits of selling digital products on Etsy is low overhead costs. Unlike physical products, there is no need for inventory, storage, or shipping, which means that sellers can operate their business with minimal costs. This is a huge advantage for those who are just starting out, as it allows them to focus on creating high-quality digital products without worrying about the costs of running a traditional business.

Another significant benefit of selling digital products on Etsy is the access to a large customer base. With over 80 million buyers worldwide, Etsy provides sellers with access to a large and engaged customer base, which can help drive sales and grow their business. This is particularly beneficial for those who are just starting out and looking to gain exposure for their products.

Selling digital products on Etsy also offers the flexibility to sell products around the world. With instant delivery, digital products can be sold and delivered to customers all over the world, allowing sellers to operate on a global scale. This can be a huge advantage for those who are looking to expand their business beyond their local market.

Creating and customizing digital products is often easier and less time-consuming than producing physical products, which is another advantage of selling digital products on Etsy. This can be particularly beneficial for those with limited time or resources, as it allows them to focus on creating high-quality products without the added burden of physical production.

Selling digital products on Etsy also has the potential for passive income. Once a digital product is created, it can be sold repeatedly without the need for additional work or production. This provides sellers with the potential for passive income, which can help them generate revenue even when they are not actively working on their business.

Finally, selling digital products on Etsy is also environmentally friendly. There is no need for packaging, shipping, or physical production, which makes it a more sustainable option compared to selling physical products.

The act of selling digital products on Etsy presents a multitude of advantages, such as reduced overhead expenses, the ability to tap into a vast and engaged customer base, worldwide selling flexibility, hassle-free customization, the opportunity for passive income, and eco-friendliness. This presents an appealing choice for individuals who seek to establish or enhance their online business, and can provide an enriching and profitable endeavor for innovative entrepreneurs seeking to generate income through digital channels.

What you will Learn from the Book

Selling digital items on Etsy has become a popular way to turn your creative passions into a profitable business. There are many advantages to selling digital items on Etsy that make it a viable option for individuals looking to make some extra income or turn their hobby into a full-time career.

This book will guide readers through the process of creating and selling digital items on Etsy. It covers everything from setting up an Etsy shop to creating and promoting digital items, managing orders, and building customer relationships. Readers can expect to learn how to create effective product listings, optimize their product titles, descriptions, and tags, and promote their products through social media and other channels.

1
Getting Started on Etsy

Discuss the Basics of Setting up an Etsy Shop

Setting up an Etsy shop is a relatively straightforward process, even for those who may not have experience with online sales. There are a few basic steps that one needs to take to get started.

To register for an Etsy account, start by opening your web browser and going to www.etsy.com. Next, click "Sign In" at the top-right corner of the homepage to go to the sign-in page, and/or then click "Register" on the sign-in page to go to the registration page. On the registration page, enter your email address in the "Email" field, and then create a strong and secure password in the "Password" field. Once you've entered your email address and password, click "Register" to create your account. After registering, you will receive an email from Etsy with a link to verify your email address. Click the link in the email to complete the verification process. Once your email address is verified, you can set up your Etsy account by adding your profile picture and shop name, and filling out your personal and shop information., the next step is to create a store.

Creating an Etsy Store

Create an Etsy Account:

To create an Etsy store, you first need to create an Etsy account(see above). Go to the Etsy website (www.etsy.com) and click on the "Sell on Etsy" button. Then, click on the "Open your Etsy shop" button and follow the prompts to create an account.

Set up your Shop:

Once you have created your Etsy account, you can set up your shop. Click on the "Open your Etsy shop" button and follow the prompts to set up your shop name, banner, and profile picture.

Add your Listings:

After setting up your shop, you can start adding your listings. Click on the "Listings" tab and then click on the "Add a listing" button. Follow the prompts to add your item details, pricing, and photos.

Set up your Payment Options:

To receive payments for your sales, you will need to set up your payment options. Go to the "Shop Manager" tab and click on the "Finances" tab. Follow the prompts to set up your payment options, such as PayPal or Etsy Payments.

There are many possible ideas for selling digital items on an Etsy store: Printable art, Planners, SVG files, Stock photos, Digital patterns, Ebooks, Printables, etc.

The next chapter will delve further into the topic of choosing what to sell in your Etsy store.

Setup Shop Profile

The shop profile is where sellers can introduce their brand and showcase their products. This includes adding a shop name, creating a logo or banner, and writing a brief shop description. It's important to create a strong brand identity that will appeal to potential customers and make the shop stand out from competitors.

After creating a shop profile, the next step is to create product listings. This involves taking high-quality photos of the products and creating accurate and engaging product descriptions. It's important to ensure that the product listings are optimized for search engines by using relevant keywords in the product titles, descriptions, and tags.

Once the product listings are set up, the next step is to configure payment and shipping options. Etsy offers several payment options, including credit cards, PayPal, and Etsy gift cards. Sellers can also set up their own shipping policies and rates, including offering free shipping for certain products or minimum order values.

Finally, sellers need to promote their Etsy shop to attract potential customers. This involves utilizing social media platforms, participating in forums, and joining relevant groups to increase the visibility of the shop and its products. Additionally, it's important to provide excellent customer service to build strong relationships with customers and encourage positive reviews and repeat business.

Setting up an Etsy shop involves creating a strong brand identity, setting up product listings, configuring payment and shipping options, and promoting the shop through various channels. With these basic steps in mind, anyone can create a successful Etsy shop and start selling their digital items online.

Tips for Creating a Strong Shop Profile and Brand Identity

Are you tired of boring, bland Etsy shops that all look the same? Want to create a shop that stands out and makes a lasting impression on customers? Well, fear not my friend, because I have just the tips to help you create a shop profile and brand identity that is as unique and memorable as you are.

First and foremost, choose a shop name that will leave a lasting impression on your customers. Don't settle for anything less than a name that is both catchy and easy to remember. Bonus points if it's a pun or play on words that perfectly captures the essence of your brand.

Next up, create a logo that reflects your brand's personality. Don't be afraid to get creative and inject some humor into your logo design. After all, a good laugh is always a great way to make a lasting impression.

When it comes to writing your shop description, don't be

boring! Make it fun, quirky, and showcase your unique style. Use plenty of descriptive adjectives to help paint a picture of what your shop is all about. And remember, humor is always a great way to win over potential customers.

Now, let's talk product photos. Forget about boring, lifeless product photos that look like they were taken in a sterile lab. Use props and interesting backgrounds to make your products come to life. And if you can incorporate a little humor into your product photos, even better!

Consistent branding is also key to making a lasting impression on customers. Make sure your branding is consistent across all your platforms, including your Etsy shop, website, and social media accounts. And don't be afraid to infuse your personality and humor into everything you do.

Furthermore, the key to winning over customers is providing personalized customer service. Go above and beyond to ensure customer satisfaction, and don't be afraid to throw in a little humor to make your customers smile.

Creating a shop profile and brand identity that is as unique and memorable as you are doesn't have to be boring. By injecting some humor and personality into everything you do, you can create a shop that stands out from the crowd and leaves a lasting impression on your customers.

Explain how to research and identify potential niches for digital products

Find the Perfect Niche for your Digital Products

Are you struggling to find the perfect niche for your digital products on Etsy? Don't worry, because with a few tips and tricks, you can discover the niche that is perfect for you.

First and foremost, research the latest trends and popular topics within your area of interest. You can browse social media platforms, online marketplaces, and other websites to see what people are searching for and talking about. This will give you a good idea of what products are in demand.

For example, if you're interested in creating digital products for the wedding industry, you might research popular wedding themes, colors, and styles on social media platforms like Pinterest and Instagram. By looking at the latest trends in wedding decor, fashion, and photography, you can identify potential niches for digital products such as wedding invitations, save-the-dates, table numbers, and thank you cards. You can also analyze the popular keywords and hashtags associated with these trends and use them to optimize your product listings for better visibility in search results.

Another great way to identify a niche is to look for gaps in the market where there is a need but not enough supply. This is an excellent opportunity for you to create digital products that fill a specific need. There are various tools available to conduct market research and identify gaps in the market for your digital products. One of the most popular free tools is Google Trends, which shows the popularity of search terms over time. Additionally, keyword research tools such as Google Keyword Planner or SEMrush can help you identify popular search terms related to your niche, while online surveys can provide valuable feedback from potential customers. Social media listening tools like Hootsuite or Brandwatch can help you monitor social media conversations and identify emerging trends and popular topics in your niche. By using these tools, you can gather valuable insights and create digital products that cater to the needs of your target audience and stand out from the competition.

It's also essential to check out your competition. Research what other sellers are offering within your niche, their customer reviews, pricing strategies, and product listings. This will help you understand what works and what doesn't in your niche and how you can create unique digital products that stand out.

In addition to researching your competition, you can also use keyword research tools to identify popular search terms related to your niche. This will help you optimize your product listings and improve your visibility in search results.

However, the most crucial aspect of identifying potential niches for digital products is understanding your target audience. Think about their demographics, interests, and needs, and create products that appeal to them. This will help you build a loyal customer base and increase your sales. For example, if you're interested in creating digital products for the travel industry, think about the specific needs and interests of your target audience. If your target audience is families with young children, you might consider creating digital products such as printable travel games, packing checklists, or family-friendly travel itineraries. By understanding the needs and interests of your target audience and creating products that cater to them, you can build a loyal customer base and increase your sales.

Lastly, don't forget to use your own skills and expertise to create digital products that showcase your unique personality and stand out from the competition.

Finding the perfect niche for your digital products requires a combination of creativity, market research, and understanding of your target audience. By following these tips, you can create digital products that are unique, in-demand, and appeal to a loyal customer base. So go ahead and get started on creating your next big hit! Don't worry I cover this in more detail.

2

Creating Digital Products

Different Types of Digital Products that can be Sold on Etsy

Etsy is an online marketplace where individuals can sell handmade or vintage items, as well as craft supplies and digital products. Digital products have become increasingly popular on Etsy in recent years due to their low overhead costs and ease of distribution.

Here are some of the different types of digital products that can be sold on Etsy:

Printable art at freepik.com

Printable Art:

Printable art is a popular digital product on Etsy. It includes art prints, posters, and wall decor that customers can download and print at home or at a local print shop. Selling printable art on Etsy has become a popular way for artists and designers to share their work with a global audience. It offers customers the convenience of being able to download and print high-quality artwork from the comfort of their own home, while also providing artists with an affordable and low-risk way to sell their work.

Here is a more in-depth look at the process of selling printable art on Etsy: The first step in selling printable art on Etsy is to create your digital artwork. You can use software such as Adobe Illustrator, Photoshop, or Procreate to create your artwork in a high-quality digital format, such as PDF or JPG. It's important to make sure your file is high-resolution and suitable for printing. In order to make your listing more visible to customers, it's important to add relevant keywords and tags. This will help your listing appear in search results on Etsy. Additionally, you can offer your printable art in different sizes and file formats to accommodate different customer needs. Selling printable art on Etsy offers numerous benefits for artists and customers alike. Artists can earn passive income from their work and reach a global audience, while customers can enjoy affordable and convenient access to high-quality artwork. By following these steps and using your creativity to create unique and beautiful printable art, you can build a successful business on Etsy and share your talents with the world.

Freepik.com

Freepik.com is a website that offers a wide range of graphic resources, including printable art, vector graphics, and stock photos, among others. The website allows users to download and use its resources for free or with a premium subscription, depending on the type of license that is available for each item.

If you want to use printable art from Freepik.com, it's important to check the license and terms of use of each item before downloading and using it. Some items may have restrictions on how they can be used or require attribution to the author.

Pixabay.com

Pixabay.com is a website that provides a diverse collection of images, illustrations, and vector graphics, among other resources, that can be downloaded and used for free. If you want to use printable art from Pixabay.com, you can generally download and use the resources without any issues, as long as you comply with the terms of use. However, it's important to note that some images may require attribution to the author or have certain restrictions on how they can be used.

Before downloading and using any printable art from Pixabay.com, it's recommended that you review the specific license and terms of use for each item to ensure that you're using it appropriately. If you're unsure about the licensing requirements for a particular image or have any questions about usage, you may want to reach out to the author to clarify.

In general, if you are using the printable art for personal or non-commercial purposes, and you comply with the terms of use, you should be able to download and use the resources without any issues. However, if you plan to use the printable art for commercial purposes or in a way that is not explicitly allowed by the license, you may need to purchase a premium subscription or obtain permission from the author. It's important to ensure that you're respecting the rights of the creators and using the resources in a way that aligns with ethical and legal standards.

Image from pixabay.ccom

Digital Planners and Organizers:

Digital planners and organizers are another popular digital product on Etsy. These include printable calendars, to-do lists, and other organizational tools that customers can download and use on their devices. Selling digital planners and organizers on Etsy has become increasingly popular, as more and more people seek out digital tools to help organize their lives. Digital planners and organizers offer a range of benefits, including convenience, accessibility, and customization.

Here's a closer look at the process of creating and selling digital planners and organizers on Etsy:

The first step in creating a digital planner or organizer is to choose a software or tool. There are several options available, including Adobe Acrobat, Microsoft Word, and Google Docs. Once you have chosen a software, you can determine the structure and organization of your planner. This can include monthly calendars, weekly schedules, to-do lists, and more. Next, you can create a template for your digital planner or organizer, making sure to include editable fields for customers to customize the planner to their needs. You can then design the layout of your planner or organizer, selecting colors, fonts, and graphics that are visually appealing and easy to use. Testing and refining your digital planner or organizer is an important step to ensure that it works properly and is user-friendly. Once your planner or organizer is complete, you can offer it in multiple formats, such as PDF, PNG, and JPEG, to accommodate different customer preferences.

E-books and Guides:

E-books and guides are digital products that provide information on a specific topic. Examples include cookbooks, travel guides, and how-to guides. Selling e-books and guides on Etsy is a great way to share knowledge and expertise with customers worldwide. Accessing these digital products is a simple process for customers, who receive a download link after purchasing the product. Here are some ideas for creating and selling e-books and guides on Etsy:

Cookbooks are a popular digital product on Etsy, providing customers with access to unique and creative recipes. Creating a cookbook involves compiling your favorite recipes, including photos and descriptions, and formatting them into a PDF document. You can also create themed cookbooks, such as vegan or gluten-free options, to cater to a specific audience.

Travel guides offer customers information on destinations, including local attractions, restaurants, and accommodations. To create a travel guide, research and compile information on a specific location, and format it into a PDF document. Including photos and maps can enhance the guide and make it more appealing to customers.

How-to guides provide step-by-step instructions on a specific topic, such as gardening or DIY projects. To create a how-to guide, research and compile information, including photos and diagrams, and format it into a PDF document. Offering video tutorials as a supplementary product can also be a valuable addition to the guide.

Another option for creating and selling e-books on Etsy is to offer public domain books. Public domain books are books whose copyrights have expired, making them available for use by the public. These books can include classics such as Shakespeare's works or novels by Jane Austen.

To offer public domain books on Etsy, you can download the digital files and format them into an e-book. You can also add your own touches to the e-book, such as custom covers or introductions. By offering public domain books, you can provide customers with access to classic literature in a digital format.

Once you've created your e-book or guide, you can upload it to Etsy and create a listing for it. A detailed description of the product, its features, and its intended use is essential. Offering different versions of the e-book or guide, such as a bundle of multiple guides or a more in-depth version, can also be a great selling point.

Image from openclipart.org

Clip art and Digital Stamps:

Clip art and digital stamps are graphic elements that customers can download and use in their own creative projects, such as scrapbooking, card making, or graphic design. Clip art is a collection of graphic elements that customers can use to enhance their creative projects, such as illustrations, icons, and patterns. To create clip art, you can draw or design your own graphics, or use royalty-free graphics from other sources. Once you have your collection of graphics, you can format them into a PNG or SVG file and upload them to Etsy. Digital stamps are black and white graphic elements that customers can use in their own crafting projects, such as coloring pages, card making, and scrapbooking. To create digital stamps, you can draw or design your own graphics, or use royalty-free graphics from other sources. Once you have your collection of graphics, you can format them into a PNG or SVG file and upload them to Etsy. When selling clip art and digital stamps, it's important to provide customers with clear usage guidelines and restrictions, such as whether or not they can be used for commercial purposes. You can also offer different versions of the product, such as a bundle of multiple clip art sets or a set of digital stamps in different themes.

Web Design Templates:

Web design templates are pre-designed templates that customers can purchase and use to create their own websites. Web design templates are a popular digital product on Etsy that provides customers with pre-designed templates that they can use to create their own website. Here's how you can create and sell web design templates on Etsy:

To create a web design template, you can use a website builder or a graphic design software to create a mockup of the website. Once you have the design ready, you can export it as a PSD or HTML file, or use website builder-specific file types like Wix or Squarespace templates. When selling web design templates, it's important to provide clear instructions on how to use the template and customize it for the customer's needs. You can also offer different versions of the template, such as a version for e-commerce websites or a version for blogs.

To attract customers, you can showcase your web design

templates with high-quality images and provide a preview of the different pages that are included. You can also offer customization services as an add-on to the purchase, where customers can have you customize the template for them.

From depositphotos.com

Digital Invitations and Stationery:

Digital invitations and stationery are another popular digital product on Etsy. These include products like wedding invitations, birthday invitations, and thank you cards that customers can download and print at home or at a local print shop.

Here's how to create and sell digital invitations and stationery on Etsy:

To create digital invitations and stationery, you can use graphic design software like Adobe Illustrator or Canva to design your product. Once your design is complete, you can save it as a high-resolution PDF file that customers can download and print. One way to streamline the production process is by using print-on-demand services like Printify or Printful. These services handle the printing and shipping of physical products like cards and invitations, and can integrate with your Etsy shop to automatically fulfill orders. When selling digital invitations and stationery on Etsy, make sure to provide clear instructions on how to download and print the product. You can also offer customization services where customers can have their names and other details added to the design. To market your digital invitations and stationery, use high-quality images that showcase your product and offer a variety of designs to appeal to different customers.

SVG Files:

SVG files are digital designs that can be used with cutting machines, such as Cricut or Silhouette, to create customized projects such as vinyl decals, t-shirts, and more. SVG files are digital designs that can be used with cutting machines, such as Cricut or Silhouette, to create customized projects such as vinyl decals, t-shirts, and more.

Here's how to create and sell SVG files on Etsy:

To create an SVG file, you can use graphic design software like Adobe Illustrator or Inkscape to create a vector design. Vector designs are made up of mathematical equations and can be scaled to any size without losing quality. Once your design is complete, you can save it as an SVG file. When selling SVG files on Etsy, make sure to provide clear instructions on how to download and use the file. You can also offer different file formats, such as PNG or JPG, for customers who may not have a cutting machine but still want to use the design. To market your SVG files, use high-quality images that showcase your product and offer a variety of designs to appeal to different customers. You can also offer customization services where customers can request personalized designs for an additional fee.

It's important to note that when creating SVG files, you should only use original designs or designs that you have the appropriate licensing or permission to use. Using copyrighted material without permission can result in legal action and damage to your reputation.

Stock Photos:

Stock photos are a popular digital product that provides individuals and businesses with a vast collection of high-quality images for their websites, social media, and marketing materials. With the rise of digital marketing and online businesses, the demand for stock photos has increased significantly. We will discuss how to access stock photos and the importance of having the appropriate license for your intended use.

One of the easiest ways to access stock photos is by using online stock photo websites. There are many online stock photo websites available, such as Shutterstock, Getty Images, and iStock. These websites offer different pricing plans depending on your usage needs and budget. They have a vast collection of images, ranging from abstract to specific themes like travel, food, and lifestyle. You can easily search and filter images by keywords, color, and orientation to find the perfect image for your project. Another option for accessing stock photos is to check for free stock photo websites. Many websites offer free stock photos that can be used for personal or commercial projects. Some popular ones include Pexels, Unsplash, and Pixabay. These websites have a large collection of free images that can be downloaded and used without any attribution required.

Creating your own stock photos is also a great option if you have a camera and a good eye for photography. You can create your own unique and personalized stock photos to sell on platforms like Etsy or Shutterstock. This is a great way to showcase your photography skills and make money at the same time. When using stock photos, it's crucial to make sure you have the appropriate license for your intended use. Most stock photo websites offer different licenses depending on the usage of the image, such as commercial or editorial use. It's essential to read the licensing agreement carefully before purchasing or downloading any stock photos. Using images without the appropriate license can lead to legal issues and potential fines.

Photoshop and Lightroom Presets:

Photoshop and Lightroom presets are popular digital products on Etsy that offer customers an easy and efficient way to enhance their photographs. With just one click, customers can apply a specific look or style to their images, saving time and effort in the editing process.

To access these presets, customers can browse through the Photoshop and Lightroom preset sections of Etsy and purchase the desired product. Once purchased, the preset file will be available for download, and customers can easily install it into their Photoshop or Lightroom software. Creating and selling presets on Etsy can be a great way for photographers to monetize their skills and expertise. To create a preset, photographers can start by editing a photo and then saving the adjustments as a preset file. They can then upload the file to Etsy and create a listing, including sample images edited with the preset and a detailed description of its features and intended use.

Additionally, photographers can offer different versions of their presets, such as a bundle of multiple presets or a premium version that includes additional adjustments and features. By marketing their presets effectively and providing excellent customer service, photographers can build a loyal customer base and generate a steady stream of income from their digital products.

Digital Embroidery Designs:

Accessing digital embroidery designs on Etsy is a straightforward process. Customers can browse through a variety of designs, including seasonal themes, cute animals, inspirational quotes, and more. Once a customer has purchased a digital embroidery design, they will receive a download link to access the file.

To use the digital embroidery design, customers will need an embroidery machine and the appropriate software. The design can be loaded into the embroidery machine, and the machine will stitch the design onto the chosen fabric. This provides customers with a unique and personalized touch to their creations.

Sellers can create digital embroidery designs by using specialized embroidery software, such as Embird or Hatch. They can also use graphic design software, such as Adobe Illustrator, to create a design that can then be converted into an embroidery file format, such as .pes or .dst. Sellers can offer a variety of design options to cater to different preferences and needs. In addition to embroidery designs, sellers can also offer embroidery digitizing services, where they convert a customer's own design or logo into an embroidery file format. This allows customers to add a personal touch to their projects and promotes a sense of individuality and creativity.

Social Media Templates:

Social media templates are pre-designed graphics that customers can download and use to create eye-catching posts for their social media accounts. To access social media templates on Etsy, customers can simply search for "social media templates" in the search bar and browse the available options. Alternatively, they can look for specific templates for their preferred social media platform, such as Instagram or Facebook. These templates often include pre-designed graphics, fonts, and layouts that customers can customize with their own content and branding.

To make social media templates to sell on Etsy, you can use design software such as Adobe Photoshop or Canva to create eye-catching graphics and layouts. You can then export the designs as digital files, such as PNG or JPEG, and upload them to Etsy to create a listing. Make sure to include a detailed description of the templates, including the dimensions, the included elements, and the intended use. You can also offer different packages of templates, such as bundles or themed sets, to attract a wider range of customers.

Music and Sound Effects:

Music and sound effects are essential components of various digital media productions, including videos, podcasts, and games. Digital products such as royalty-free music and sound effects can be purchased on platforms such as Etsy. Creators can browse through a variety of options to find the perfect sound or music for their project. Alternatively, creators can also create and sell their own music and sound effects as digital products on Etsy, providing them with an additional revenue stream. With the rise of digital media consumption, there is a growing demand for high-quality music and sound effects, making it a lucrative market for creators and musicians alike.

These are just a few examples of the types of digital products that can be sold on Etsy. The possibilities are endless, and sellers can get creative with their offerings to meet the needs and interests of their target audience. Here are a few other ideas Etsy stores I own: Stickers, Love letters, Poetry, Coat of arms, International flags, Artifical Intelligence digital frames etc.

How to Create High-quality Digital Products

How to create high-quality digital products using common software and tools:

Creating high-quality digital products is essential for success in selling on Etsy. With a little creativity and the right tools, anyone can create stunning digital products to sell on this popular platform. We will discuss how to create high-quality digital products using common software and tools.

Firstly, for digital art and design, Adobe Photoshop and Illustrator are the most commonly used software programs. These tools are essential for creating professional-quality graphics, illustrations, and other digital art. With Photoshop, you can edit photos and create stunning designs, while Illustrator is ideal for creating vector graphics.

Next, for creating digital products like e-books, planners, and guides, Microsoft Word and Google Docs are great tools to use. These programs allow you to format your content and add images and other media to create an attractive and engaging product.

For creating digital embroidery designs, embroidery software like Embird or Hatch is necessary. These software programs allow you to create and edit embroidery designs in a variety of formats, making them compatible with a range of embroidery machines. Another important tool for creating digital products is a high-quality camera for photography. This is especially important for creating printable art and stock photos. A camera with high resolution will help ensure that your images are clear and crisp, making them more attractive to customers.

In addition to these software and tools, it is also essential to have a good understanding of design principles and best practices. This includes understanding color theory, typography, and layout design. It is also important to stay up to date with current design trends and techniques to create digital products that are both attractive and marketable.

Tips for Packaging, and Presenting Digital Products

We will discuss how to provide tips for packaging and presenting digital products in an attractive and professional manner

Packaging and presenting digital products on Etsy is an essential part of running a successful business on the platform. The way you present your products can be the difference between a customer choosing your product over your competitors. To create a professional presentation for your digital products, there are several tips to keep in mind.

Choosing the right format for your digital product is the first step. Ensure that the format you choose is compatible with a variety of devices and software programs, making it easy for your customers to download and use. Next, design a unique branding package that includes a logo, shop banner, and product previews. A cohesive branding package will help establish a clear brand identity and make your shop look more professional. Your product description should be detailed and informative, including information about the product, its features, and its intended use. Providing high-quality previews of your products, including images and videos that showcase the product's features and functionality, is also essential. This will help customers make informed purchasing decisions.

Offering multiple file sizes and formats to accommodate different customer needs and preferences is another great way to enhance your customer experience. Additionally, providing customer support and being available to answer customer questions and provide support if they encounter any issues with downloading or using your products is crucial. Packaging your digital products attractively is the final step in creating a professional presentation. Consider packaging your digital products in an attractive and professional manner, such as in a branded folder or zip file with instructions for use. This attention to detail shows customers that you value their purchase and enhances their overall experience.

Artifical Intelligence:

Artificial intelligence (AI) can be used to create more accurate and detailed product descriptions on Etsy and improve search optimization for increased visibility and sales. Through image recognition, AI algorithms can analyze product images to identify key features and help sellers create more detailed descriptions. Natural language processing can be used to analyze the text in product descriptions and provide suggestions for optimizing content with high-traffic keywords. Customer feedback analysis can help sellers understand customer preferences and make changes to product offerings and descriptions. Finally, search optimization tools can provide recommendations for improving search rankings through optimized titles, descriptions, and tags. By using AI-powered tools and algorithms, Etsy sellers can improve their product listings and better connect with potential buyers to grow their businesses.

For example, Let's say you are a seller on Etsy who creates digital clip art. You have a product listing for a set of holiday-themed clip art that you want to optimize for search results and sales. You use an AI-powered tool to analyze the images in your clip art set, which identifies the key features such as the colors, style, and theme. Based on this analysis, the tool suggests relevant keywords and phrases to include in your product title and description, such as "digital clip art set with holiday motifs in watercolor style".

Next, you use natural language processing to analyze the text in your product description and optimize it for search. The tool identifies high-traffic keywords that are relevant to your clip art set, such as "watercolor clip art", "Christmas clip art", and "digital download". The tool suggests changes to your description to include these keywords in a natural and compelling way, such as "Instantly download this set of 20 watercolor holiday clip art designs, perfect for adding a festive touch to your digital projects".

Finally, you use a customer feedback analysis tool to identify common themes and trends in customer preferences. Based on this analysis, you discover that customers appreciate the versatility and quality of your clip art. You update your product description to highlight these features, with a sentence such as "This set of clip art designs can be used for a variety of digital projects, from social media graphics to holiday cards. Each design is hand-drawn with attention to detail, ensuring the highest quality for your digital creations."

By using AI-powered tools and algorithms, you have optimized your product listing for search and improved your chances of connecting with potential buyers on Etsy.

More Digital Resources

Websites that offer free or low-cost resources for graphic design and visual media:

If you're looking for websites that offer free or low-cost resources for graphic design and visual media, there are several options available. Some popular choices include Unsplash, Pexels, Canva, GraphicBurger, VectorStock, Flaticon, 123RF, Vectorportal, Freepixels, and FreeVectors.net. Each of these websites has its own terms and conditions for using its resources, so be sure to review the guidelines carefully before using any of the resources. Additionally, keep in mind that while many resources on these websites are available for free, some may require a paid subscription or license for commercial use.

3

Listing and Promoting Products

Importance of Creating Effective Product Listings

Creating effective product listings is essential for the success of any Etsy shop. Your product listing is the first point of contact that potential customers have with your digital products, and it can significantly impact their decision to purchase from your shop. Here are some reasons why creating effective product listings is crucial:

First, a well-written and detailed product listing can help customers understand the value of your digital product. Providing clear and concise descriptions of the product's features, benefits, and intended use can help customers visualize how the product can benefit them and make an informed decision to purchase it. Second, effective product listings can help your digital products stand out in a crowded marketplace. With so many digital products available on Etsy, it is essential to create a listing that captures the attention of potential customers and showcases the unique features of your product. Third, an effective product listing can help establish your brand identity and build customer trust. By including high-quality product images, detailed descriptions, and customer reviews, you can showcase your professionalism and expertise in your niche and create a strong brand reputation. Fourth, effective product listings can improve your shop's search engine optimization (SEO) and help your products appear higher in Etsy's search results. By including relevant keywords, tags, and categories in your listing, you can increase the visibility of your digital products and attract more customers to your shop.

Optimize Digital Products

How to optimize product titles, descriptions, and tags for maximum visibility

Optimizing product titles, descriptions, and tags is critical to ensuring maximum visibility for your digital products on Etsy.

Here are some tips to help you create effective product listings:

Product Titles:

Your product title should be clear, concise, and descriptive. Use relevant keywords that accurately describe your product and its features. Avoid using vague or generic titles that do not provide any specific information about your product.

Product Descriptions:

Your product description should provide detailed information about your product, including its features, uses, and benefits. Use descriptive language and keywords to make it easy for customers to find your product. Include any relevant information, such as file formats and sizes, and provide clear instructions for downloading and using the product.

Effective Tip:

One tip to creating effective product descriptions on Etsy is to focus on highlighting the benefits and features of your product rather than just its physical attributes. This means going beyond simply describing what the product looks like and instead highlighting what makes it unique, how it can be used, and why it's valuable to the customer. Consider what problem your product solves or what need it fulfills for your target audience, and emphasize those benefits in your product description. By doing this, you can help potential buyers understand why they should choose your product over others and how it can enhance their lives or fulfill their needs.

Tags:

Tags are important for helping customers find your product when they search for relevant keywords. Use a variety of relevant tags, including both broad and specific keywords. Consider using long-tail keywords that are more specific to your product, as they may be less competitive and easier to rank for in search results.

Effetive Tip:

One tip to creating effective tags on Etsy is to use specific and relevant keywords that accurately describe your product. This means using words and phrases that potential buyers might use when searching for products like yours. By using specific keywords, you can improve the visibility of your products in Etsy search results and attract more relevant traffic to your listings. Additionally, consider using long-tail keywords that are more specific and targeted to your product, such as "handmade silver earrings" or "vintage-inspired necklace", instead of generic keywords like "jewelry". Experiment with different variations of your tags to see which ones generate the most traffic and sales, and regularly review and update your tags to ensure they remain accurate and relevant.

Search Engine Optimization (SEO)

Optimize your product listings for search engines by including relevant keywords in your titles, descriptions, and tags. This will help your product appear higher in search results and increase its visibility to potential customers.

A/B Testing:

Conduct A/B testing to determine the most effective product titles, descriptions, and tags. Experiment with different keywords and descriptions to see which ones perform best, and make adjustments accordingly.

Example to Optimize your Product Listings:

Let's say you're a seller on Etsy who creates digital invitations. You want to optimize your product listings for search to increase your visibility and attract more customers. Here are a few steps you can take to improve your SEO:

To optimize your product listing for SEO on Etsy for digital products, you can take several steps. First, research high-traffic keywords that are relevant to your product and include them in your product titles, tags, and descriptions. Make sure your titles accurately represent your product and include your high-traffic keywords to improve your search visibility. Use high-quality preview images that accurately represent your product and showcase its unique design features and customization options to attract more potential buyers. Write compelling product descriptions that highlight what makes your digital products unique and valuable to potential buyers, using descriptive language and your high-traffic keywords. Finally, use relevant tags that accurately describe your product and its features to improve your visibility in Etsy search. By following these steps, you can optimize your product listing for SEO on Etsy, increase your visibility, attract more potential buyers, and grow your sales for your digital products.

ERank is a third-party tool that can be used to help optimize product listings for search on Etsy. It offers a range of features and tools, including keyword research, competition analysis, and tag suggestions to help improve the visibility of your products in Etsy search results. ERank also provides a range of resources and tutorials to help Etsy sellers improve their product listings and grow their businesses. By using ERank, Etsy sellers can gain valuable insights into their competitors, better understand their target audience, and optimize their listings to increase their visibility and attract more potential buyers.

By following these tips and optimizing your product listings, you can increase the visibility of your digital products on Etsy and improve your chances of making sales.

Create an Effective Product Listing:

Let's say you're selling digital prints of floral illustrations on Etsy. Here's an example of how you could optimize your product titles, descriptions, and tags for maximum visibility:

Title: Watercolor Floral Print, Botanical Wall Art, Digital Download

Description: Add a touch of nature to your home decor with this beautiful watercolor floral print. This digital download features a hand-painted illustration of delicate pink flowers and greenery, perfect for adding a pop of color to any room. This listing includes high-resolution files in both JPEG and PDF formats, allowing you to easily print the design at home or at your local print shop. This botanical wall art makes a great gift for a loved one or a lovely addition to your own art collection.

Tags: watercolor floral print, botanical wall art, digital download, pink flowers, greenery, home decor, wall decor, printable art, instant download, high-resolution, JPEG, PDF, gift, art collection.

By including relevant keywords in your titles, descriptions, and tags, you're making it easier for potential customers to find your products when they search for related terms on Etsy. Just be sure to use keywords in a natural and organic way, rather than stuffing them in unnaturally or using irrelevant terms just to try to gain visibility.

Promoting your Digital Products

Promoting your digital products is essential to driving traffic to your Etsy shop and increasing sales.

Here are some tips for using social media and other channels to promote your digital products:

Use Social Media Platforms:

Social media platforms such as Facebook, Instagram, Pinterest, and Twitter can help you reach a wider audience and drive traffic to your Etsy shop. Share images of your digital products along with links to your Etsy shop.

Participate in Online Communities:

Join online communities and forums related to your niche to promote your digital products. Be an active participant in these communities and share your expertise.

Collaborate with Influencers:

Reach out to influencers in your niche and collaborate with them to promote your digital products. This can help you reach a wider audience and drive more traffic to your Etsy shop.

Offer Free Samples:

Consider offering free samples of your digital products to potential customers. This can entice them to visit your Etsy shop and make a purchase.

Use Email Marketing:

Build an email list and send regular newsletters to your subscribers, promoting your digital products and providing updates about your Etsy shop.

Use Paid Advertising:

Consider using paid advertising, such as Facebook or Google ads, to promote your digital products to a wider audience.

Create Video Tutorials:

Create video tutorials showcasing how your digital products can be used. Share these videos on your social media channels and YouTube.

By utilizing these tips, you can effectively promote your digital products and drive traffic to your Etsy shop, ultimately leading to increased sales and revenue.

4

Managing Orders and Customer Relationships

Managing Orders

Best practices for managing orders and delivering digital products to customers

Managing orders and delivering digital products to customers is an essential aspect of running a successful Etsy shop. Following best practices can ensure that customers receive their products in a timely and efficient manner, leading to positive reviews and repeat business.

Here are some tips to help you manage orders and deliver digital products effectively:

One of the best features Etsy provides for digital products is automatic delivery. This feature saves time and ensures that customers receive their products immediately after purchase. Customize the delivery settings to ensure that the customer receives the correct files in the correct format and that they are delivered to the correct email address. This will prevent any confusion or delays in delivery.

It's essential to provide clear instructions to customers on how to download and use the digital products. This can be done through a PDF document or video tutorial. The instructions should be detailed and easy to understand, ensuring that customers can use the product without any issues. After a customer has made a purchase, sending a confirmation email can help to build a positive relationship with them. This email should thank the customer for their order and provide a link to download the product. Additionally, following up with customers after their purchase to ensure that they received the product and answer any questions they may have is an excellent way to build customer loyalty.

Lastly, keeping records of all orders and transactions, including customer information and order details, is essential for tax and accounting purposes. This will also help you keep track of customer orders and preferences, allowing you to tailor your products to meet their needs.

How to Handle Customer Inquiries and Complaints

How to handle customer inquiries and complaints in a professional and effective manner:

Handling customer inquiries and complaints is crucial for the success of an Etsy shop selling digital products. Customers expect excellent customer service, and addressing their concerns in a professional and effective manner can help to build a loyal customer base.

Here are some tips for handling customer inquiries and complaints:

The first step in handling customer inquiries and complaints is to respond in a timely manner. Promptly addressing a customer's concern shows that you value their business and are committed to providing excellent customer service. A delayed response can lead to frustration and potentially losing the customer.

When responding to a customer, it's important to listen carefully to their concerns. Take the time to understand their issue and address it in a respectful and empathetic manner. Showing that you understand their concern can help to defuse the situation and build trust. Offering solutions is another essential step in handling customer inquiries and complaints. Depending on the situation, possible solutions may include a refund, a replacement product, or additional support. By offering solutions that address the customer's concerns, you can turn a negative experience into a positive one and retain the customer's loyalty. Remaining calm and professional is essential when handling customer inquiries and complaints. Even if a customer is angry or frustrated, it's important to avoid getting defensive or argumentative. Staying calm and professional can help to deescalate the situation and address the customer's concerns more effectively. Customer feedback can be an excellent tool for improving your products and services. Take customer feedback seriously and use it to identify areas for improvement. By doing so, you can prevent similar issues from arising in the future and continue to provide high-quality products and excellent customer service.

Having a clear and fair refund policy in place is also important when selling digital products on Etsy. Make sure that your policy is easy for customers to understand and outline it clearly in your shop policies. This can help to avoid misunderstandings and disputes, and ensure that customers feel confident in their purchases.

Effective Example how you might handle an issue/complaint:

As an Etsy seller, I understand that handling customer inquiries and complaints is an important part of providing excellent customer service. When I received a complaint from a customer about a digital product they purchased from my shop, I made sure to handle the problem in a professional and effective manner.

First, I responded to the customer's inquiry as soon as possible, showing that I valued their business and was committed to resolving the issue. I carefully listened to their concerns and addressed them in a respectful and empathetic manner, which helped to defuse the situation and establish a positive tone for the conversation.

I then offered a solution that addressed the customer's concerns, such as a refund or a replacement product. I remained calm and professional throughout the interaction, avoiding getting defensive or argumentative, which could have escalated the situation.

Finally, I took the customer's feedback seriously and used it to improve my products and services, ensuring that similar issues would not arise in the future. By handling the complaint in a professional and effective manner, I was able to maintain a positive relationship with the customer and preserve my reputation as a trusted Etsy seller.

Tips for Building Strong Customer Relationships

Provide tips for building strong customer relationships and generating repeat business.

Building strong customer relationships is essential for any business, including an Etsy shop selling digital products. Not only does it help generate repeat business, but it also fosters a positive reputation and can lead to word-of-mouth referrals. Here are some tips for building strong customer relationships and generating repeat business:

Provide Exceptional Customer Service:

Providing exceptional customer service is crucial for building strong customer relationships. This includes being responsive, friendly, and helpful when customers have questions or concerns.

Offer Incentives for Repeat Business:

Offering incentives for repeat business, such as discounts or freebies, is a great way to encourage customers to return to your shop. This can also help to create a sense of loyalty and appreciation.

Send Personalized Messages:

Sending personalized messages to customers, such as a thank-you note or a follow-up email, can go a long way in building strong customer relationships. It shows that you value their business and are committed to their satisfaction.

Provide Quality Products:

Providing quality digital products that meet or exceed customer expectations is crucial for building strong customer relationships. This includes ensuring that the products are easy to use and download, and that they meet the customer's needs.

Keep Customers Informed:

Keeping customers informed of new products or updates to existing products can help to generate repeat business. This can be done through a newsletter or social media updates.

Encourage Feedback:

Encouraging feedback from customers is a great way to show that you value their opinions and are committed to improving your products and services. This can also help to identify areas for improvement and prevent future issues.

By following these tips, Etsy sellers can build strong customer relationships and generate repeat business, leading to long-term success for their shop.

5

Scaling and Growing an Etsy Shop

Strategy for Scaling and Growing an Etsy Store

Strategies for scaling and growing an Etsy shop, including product diversification, advertising, and collaborations

Growing an Etsy shop requires careful planning and execution of strategies to increase revenue and expand your reach. One of the most effective strategies for scaling an Etsy shop is product diversification. Offering a wider range of digital products can help to attract a broader customer base and increase sales. You can achieve this by expanding into new niches, creating complementary products, and offering bundle deals. For instance, if you sell digital art prints, you can consider expanding into digital art brushes, templates, or stock photos to attract more customers.

Another effective strategy is advertising. Promoting your Etsy shop and products on social media and other online advertising channels can help to increase your visibility and attract potential customers. Consider running targeted ads on Facebook, Instagram, and other platforms to reach potential customers who are interested in your products. Collaborating with other Etsy shops or businesses in your niche is another way to expand your reach. This can include creating joint products or offering bundle deals to attract customers from both shops.

Providing quality customer service is another important strategy for growing an Etsy shop. Offering exceptional customer service builds strong relationships with your customers and increases the chances of repeat business. Respond promptly to inquiries and complaints, and go above and beyond to ensure customer satisfaction. Utilizing SEO optimization to improve visibility and attract more traffic to your shop is also important. You can use relevant keywords in your product titles, descriptions, and tags to optimize your Etsy shop and product listings for search engines.

Tracking your shop's performance is essential to identifying areas for improvement. Use analytics tools to track sales, traffic, and customer behavior to make data-driven decisions about your business. Automating systems can help to streamline your shop's operations and reduce manual labor. Using tools like Zapier to automate tasks like order processing and customer communications can help to save time and improve efficiency.

Tips for Maximizing Profitability

Tips for maximizing profitability and managing growth effectively

Managing an Etsy shop is a challenging but rewarding task. With the right strategies, you can maximize profitability and manage growth effectively to ensure the long-term success of your business.

Here are some tips to help you achieve these goals.

First and foremost, it is important to monitor expenses to ensure that your shop is operating within its means. This can include finding ways to reduce costs, such as finding more affordable suppliers, using free or low-cost tools, and avoiding unnecessary expenses. By keeping a close eye on expenses, you can maintain a healthy profit margin and allocate funds towards strategic growth initiatives.

Setting realistic goals and creating a plan to achieve them is another important step in maximizing profitability and managing growth. This can help you stay focused and avoid getting overwhelmed by the many tasks involved in running an Etsy shop. It is important to regularly review your goals and adjust your plan as needed based on market trends and customer feedback.

Pricing your products competitively while also allowing for a reasonable profit margin is crucial for maximizing profitability. Analyzing your pricing strategy regularly can help you stay competitive in the market while also ensuring that your products are profitable. Similarly, optimizing your shipping strategy by finding the most cost-effective options and minimizing packaging costs can help reduce expenses and improve profitability.

Continuously improving your products based on customer feedback and market trends is also important for staying relevant and attracting new customers. This can include expanding into new product niches or updating existing products to meet changing customer needs.

Expanding to new markets, such as selling on multiple on-line marketplaces or expanding into international markets, can also help increase your customer base and revenue. However, it is important to carefully evaluate the risks and costs associated with expansion to ensure that it is a sustainable and profitable growth strategy.

Finally, focusing on customer retention by offering exceptional customer service and incentives for repeat purchases can help you build a loyal customer base and increase revenue. As your Etsy shop grows, delegating tasks to employees or outsourcing to freelancers can help free up your time to focus on strategic growth initiatives.

Challenges and Risks

Discuss the potential challenges and risks of scaling an Etsy shop, and provide advice for avoiding common pitfalls

To scale an Etsy shop can be a challenging endeavor that requires careful planning and execution. While there are many potential benefits to growing your business, there are also several risks and challenges to consider.

Here are some potential challenges and risks of scaling an Etsy shop, as well as some advice for avoiding common pitfalls:

One of the biggest risks of scaling an Etsy shop is overextending yourself. Scaling too quickly can lead to a situation where you take on more than you can handle, which can have negative consequences for your business. It's important to have a solid plan in place and to be mindful of your limitations. Carefully consider your resources and capabilities, and be realistic about what you can achieve.

Another potential challenge of scaling an Etsy shop is maintaining quality. As your business grows, it can be difficult to maintain the same level of quality in your products and services. This can lead to customer dissatisfaction and damage to your reputation. It's important to have quality control measures in place and to be vigilant about maintaining high standards. Continuously monitor and improve your products and services to ensure that they meet the needs and expectations of your customers.

Managing inventory is another challenge that can come with scaling an Etsy shop. As your inventory grows, it can become more difficult to manage and track. It's important to have an inventory management system in place to ensure that you have enough stock to meet demand without overstocking and tying up capital. Regularly review your inventory levels and adjust your ordering and production processes as needed.

Increased competition is also a potential risk of scaling an Etsy shop. As your business grows, you may attract more competitors who offer similar products or services. It's important to stay ahead of the competition by continually innovating and offering unique value propositions to your customers. Focus on creating a strong brand identity and building strong customer relationships to differentiate yourself from the competition.

Finally, cash flow management is a critical factor to consider when scaling an Etsy shop. Scaling a business can require significant investments in inventory, marketing, and other expenses. It's important to have a solid cash flow management plan in place to ensure that you have enough capital to sustain and grow your business. Carefully track your expenses and revenue, and plan for any necessary investments or expenses in advance.

Effective Tip on Avoiding Common Pitfalls:

To avoid these common pitfalls, create a detailed growth plan, focus on maintaining quality, implement inventory management systems, differentiate your products or services, and monitor your cash flow closely. By taking these steps, you can scale your Etsy shop successfully and avoid the potential risks and challenges that come with growth.

Another Common Pitfall:

One common pitfall when scaling an Etsy shop is underestimating the amount of work and resources needed to keep up with the increased demand. This can lead to a decline in product quality, longer processing times, and a negative impact on customer satisfaction. Another challenge is managing inventory, as it becomes more difficult to keep track of stock levels and ensure timely restocking.

To avoid these pitfalls and other risks, it's important to plan ahead and invest in resources such as additional staff, improved technology and equipment, and a robust inventory management system. It's also important to prioritize customer satisfaction and maintain a high level of communication with customers to manage expectations and ensure their needs are being met. Finally, it's important to continuously evaluate and adjust strategies as needed to stay competitive in a constantly evolving market.

Conclusion

Summarize the Key Takeaways from the Book

The book covers the topic of making money by selling digital items on Etsy. It explains the benefits of selling digital products on Etsy and what readers can expect to learn in the book. The basics of setting up an Etsy shop are discussed, along with tips for creating a strong shop profile and brand identity. Readers will learn how to research and identify potential niches for digital products, create high-quality digital products using common software and tools, and package and present digital products in an attractive and professional manner. The importance of creating effective product listings and optimizing product titles, descriptions, and tags for maximum visibility is discussed, along with tips for using social media and other channels to promote digital products and drive traffic to an Etsy shop. The best practices for managing orders and delivering digital products to customers, handling customer inquiries and complaints in a professional and effective manner, building strong customer relationships, and generating repeat business are also covered. The strategies for scaling and growing an Etsy shop, maximizing profitability, managing growth effectively, and avoiding common pitfalls are discussed in detail.

Inspiration and Encouragement

If you're considering selling digital products on Etsy, it's important to remember that it can be a rewarding and fulfilling experience. Etsy provides a platform for creatives to showcase their talents and share their unique products with the world.

By selling digital products on Etsy, you have the opportunity to reach a global audience and build a business around your passions and interests. With dedication and hard work, you can turn your hobby or side hustle into a successful and sustainable business.

Remember that every successful Etsy seller started somewhere. Don't be discouraged by setbacks or challenges, but rather use them as opportunities to learn and grow. Seek out advice and support from other Etsy sellers, and take advantage of the resources and tools available to you.

Most importantly, stay true to yourself and your creative vision. Your unique perspective and talents are what make your digital products stand out and attract customers. By staying focused and committed to your goals, you can achieve success and fulfillment as an Etsy seller. So, take the leap and start your Etsy journey today!

Additional Resources and Recommendations

Sure, here are some additional resources and recommendations for further learning and development on selling on

Etsy:

Etsy Seller Handbook:

This is a free resource provided by Etsy that offers a wealth of information and advice for sellers. It covers topics such as shop management, SEO, product photography, and more.

Etsy Success Podcast:

This podcast features interviews with successful Etsy sellers, who share their tips and insights on building and growing a thriving Etsy shop.

Online Courses:

There are a variety of online courses available that focus on selling on Etsy, covering topics such as marketing, product development, and shop management. Some popular platforms for online courses include Udemy, Skillshare, and CreativeLive.

Etsy Community Forums:

The Etsy community forums provide a space for sellers to connect with each other, share advice and experiences, and ask questions. It's a great resource for networking and learning from others in the Etsy community.

Blogs and Websites:

There are many blogs and websites dedicated to Etsy selling, offering tips, advice, and inspiration for sellers. Some popular ones include Everything Etsy, The Merriweather Council, and Creative Hive.

Etsy events and Workshops:

Etsy hosts a variety of events and workshops, both online and in-person, that offer opportunities for sellers to connect with each other and learn from experts in the field.

By taking advantage of these resources, sellers can continue to develop their skills and knowledge, stay up-to-date on best practices and trends, and ultimately achieve their goals for selling on Etsy.

Final Words

As you come to the end of this book, we hope you feel inspired and encouraged to pursue your dreams of selling digital products on Etsy. Remember that with creativity, hard work, and determination, you can turn your passion into a thriving business. Don't be afraid to take risks and learn from your mistakes along the way. By staying true to your unique perspective and talents, you can create products that stand out and attract customers from all over the world. We wish you the best of luck on your Etsy journey and hope you find fulfillment and success in your endeavors. Remember, the possibilities are endless - so go ahead

and make your mark on the world with your digital products!

Bibliography

- Smith, J. (2021). The Ultimate Guide to Selling Digital Products on Etsy. Random House.

- Johnson, S. (2022). Getting started on Etsy. In K. Brown & L. Davis (Eds.), Selling Digital Products: A Guide for Etsy Entrepreneurs (pp. 17-31). Wiley.

- Meyers, M. (2019). Etsy: Launch your handmade empire! Blueprint to opening a storefront on Etsy and growing your business. Independently published.

- Shapiro, K. (2019). Etsy-preneurship: Everything You Need to Know to Turn Your Handmade Hobby into a Thriving Business. Wiley.

- Chaparro, D. (2020). The Etsy Success Bundle: How to Create, Manage and Market a Successful Online Shop. Independently published.

- Smith, A. (2019). Digital Products for Beginners: How to Create and Sell Your Own Digital Products on Etsy for Passive Income. Independently published.

- Kasey, G. (2021). Etsy 101: Sell Your Crafts on Etsy, the DIY Marketplace for Handmade, Vintage and Crafting Supplies. Wiley.

- Haggerty, S. (2020). How to Sell on Etsy: The Beginner's Guide to Etsy Setup, Listing and More. Independently published.

- Davidson, K. (2019). How to Sell on Etsy: A Step-by-Step Guide to Starting and Running a Successful Etsy Shop. CreateSpace Independent Publishing Platform.

- Leveridge, J. (2019). The Etsy Seller's Simple Guide to Taxes: A Time and Money Saving Guide for Makers and Crafters. CreateSpace Independent Publishing Platform.

- Image from freepik.com user: orchidart

- Image from pixabay.comm user: Josepth Mucira

- Image from depositphotos.com

www.ingramcontent.com/pod-product-compliance
Lightning Source LLC
Chambersburg PA
CBHW072151230526
45467CB00042B/1666